W9-BWG-317

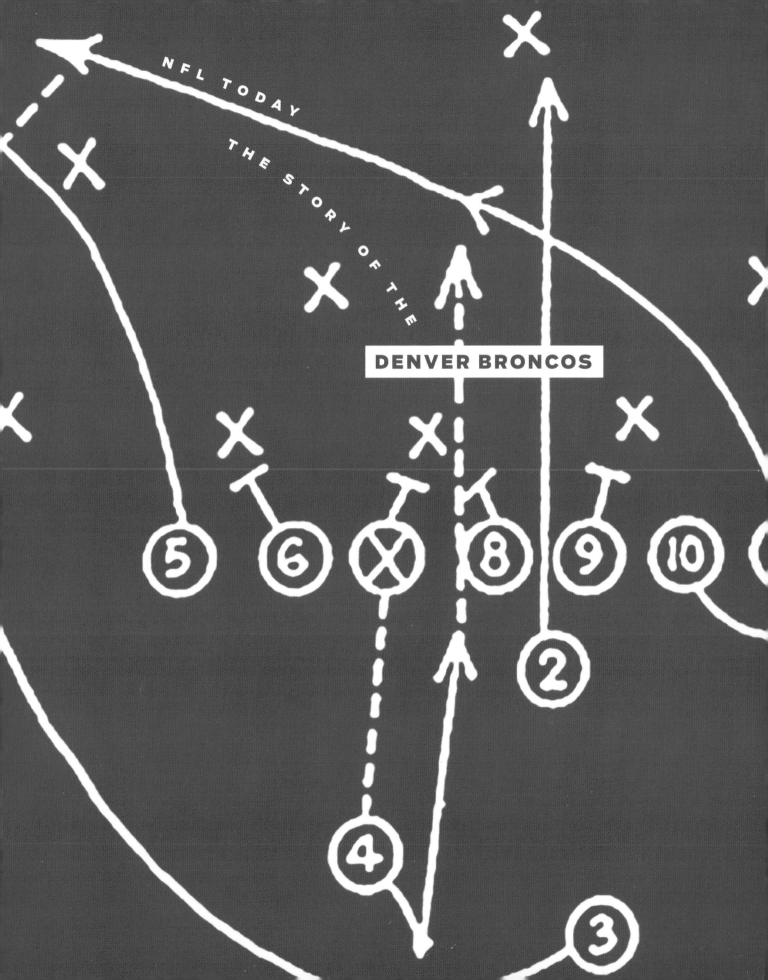

NFL TODAY

THE STORY OF THE DENVER BRONCOS

NATE FRISCH

CREATIVE EDUCATION

PUBLISHED BY CREATIVE EDUCATION
P.O. BOX 227, MANKATO, MINNESOTA 56002
CREATIVE EDUCATION IS AN IMPRINT OF THE CREATIVE COMPANY
WWW.THECREATIVECOMPANY.US

DESIGN AND PRODUCTION BY BLUE DESIGN
ART DIRECTION BY RITA MARSHALL
PRINTED IN THE UNITED STATES OF AMERICA

PHOTOGRAPHS BY CORBIS (RICH GABRIELSON/
ICON SMI), GETTY IMAGES (JAMES BALOG, HARRY
BENSON, ANDREW D. BERNSTEIN, VERNON BIEVER/
NFL, DOUG COLLIER/AFP, JONATHAN DANIEL, STEPHEN
DUNN, STEPHEN DUNN/ALLSPORT, STEVE DYKES,
JUSTIN EDMONDS, NATE FINE/NFL PHOTOS, GEORGE
GOJKOVICH, ROD HANNA/NFL, MARK LEFFINGWELL/
AFP, ANDY LYONS, AL MESSERSCHMIDT, RONALD C.
MODRA/SPORTS IMAGERY, NFL, NFL PHOTOS, DOUG
PENSINGER, DOUG PENSINGER/ALLSPORT, GEORGE
ROSE, JAMIE SQUIRE, DAMIAN STROHMEYER/SPORTS
ILLUSTRATED, GREG TROTT, RON VESELY, DILIP
VISHWANAT, CHARLES AQUA VIVA, LOU WITT/NFL)

LIBRARY OF CONGRESS CATALOGING-IN-PUBLICATION DATA
FRISCH, NATE.
THE STORY OF THE DENVER BRONCOS / BY NATE FRISCH.
P. CM. — (NFL TODAY)
INCLUDES INDEX.
SUMMARY: THE HISTORY OF THE NATIONAL FOOTBALL LEAGUE'S
DENVER BRONCOS, SURVEYING THE FRANCHISE'S BIGGEST STARS
AND MOST MEMORABLE MOMENTS FROM ITS INAUGURAL SEASON
IN 1960 TO TODAY.
ISBN 978-1-60818-301-2
1. DENVER BRONCOS (FOOTBALL TEAM)—HISTORY—JUVENILE
LITERATURE. I. TITLE.

GV956.D37F75 2012
796.332'640978883—DC23   2012031210

FIRST EDITION
9 8 7 6 5 4 3 2 1

COVER: LINEBACKER VON MILLER
PAGE 2: WIDE RECEIVER BRANDON MARSHALL
PAGES 4–5: LINEBACKER NATE WEBSTER
PAGE 6: QUARTERBACK JOHN ELWAY

TABLE OF CONTENTS

SET IN THE MOUNTAINS, DENVER IS CALLED THE "MILE-HIGH CITY"

A Slow Ascent

Nestled amid the Rocky Mountains, Denver, Colorado, began taking shape in 1858. The frontier settlement developed as a result of the Pikes Peak Gold Rush and catered mostly to miners, gamblers, and frontiersmen. But within a few years, the city primarily functioned as a center for transporting freight, livestock, passengers, and mail across the rugged and desolate mountain west. Today, Denver remains an important hub for distribution and bridges the gap between the heavily populated West Coast and cities of the Midwest. One notable change since Denver's frontier beginnings is that the mountains—once perceived as obstacles—have made the city a haven for outdoor enthusiasts such as skiers, rock climbers, and hikers.

In 1959, a different type of outdoor entertainment came to Denver when businessman Bob Howsam purchased a franchise in the newly formed American Football League (AFL). Denver's new football team was the city's first major sports franchise, and Howsam mustered early interest in the club by allowing potential fans to

DENVER BECAME A BIG-TIME SPORTS TOWN WITH THE CREATION OF THE BRONCOS

Floyd Little

RUNNING BACK / BRONCOS SEASONS: 1967–75 / HEIGHT: 5-FOOT-10 / WEIGHT: 195 POUNDS

Orange is a color that suited Floyd Little well. He first donned it as a three-time All-American halfback for the Syracuse University Orangemen, and then he pulled on a new orange jersey when he was drafted by the Denver Broncos in 1967. From the moment he signed with the Broncos, Little was known in Denver simply as "The Franchise." True to his last name, Little was a bit small at just 5-foot-10 and less than 200 pounds, but what he lacked in size he made up for in field vision and quick moves. Those moves also made Little a crucial part of the Broncos' special-teams unit as a dangerous kick returner. In 1973, The Franchise helped the Broncos attain their first winning season as they finished 7–5–2. Lou Saban, who coached the Broncos and then the Buffalo Bills, admired Little's passion. "Floyd has a driving force that no one I know can equal," he said. "He is a man. That's about as much as you can say about anybody." When the Broncos established their "Ring of Fame" in 1984, Little was one of the first inductees.

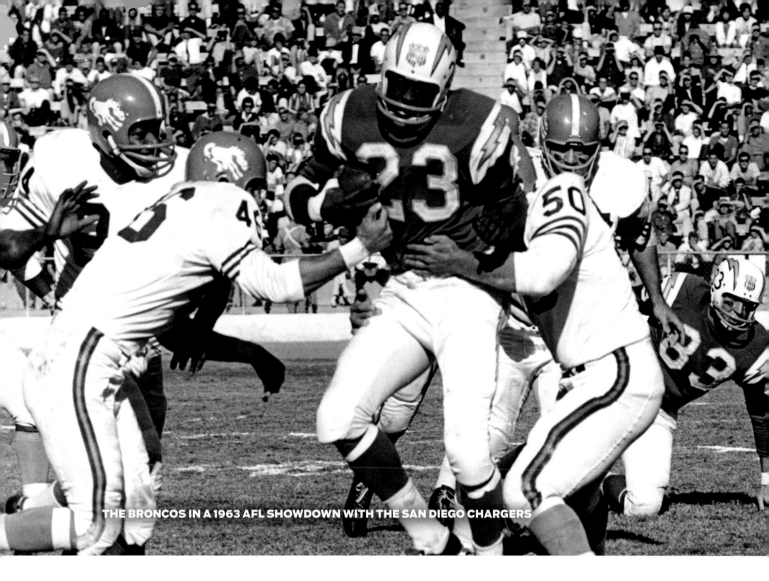

THE BRONCOS IN A 1963 AFL SHOWDOWN WITH THE SAN DIEGO CHARGERS

submit ideas for the team's name. The moniker chosen was "Broncos"—a fitting name that referred to the bucking horses that cowboys attempted to tame in Denver's bygone "Wild West" days.

When the Broncos set foot on the field for their first game in 1960, they did so in appalling uniforms. Purchased secondhand from a college team, the Broncos' threads combined drab jerseys and pants with vertically striped socks—all in brown and yellow. Fashionable or not, Denver won its inaugural game, defeating the Boston Patriots 13–10.

Despite the promising start, the Broncos were often tamed during the rest of their first season. With the exceptions of ballhawking safety Austin "Goose" Gonsoulin and sure-handed end Lionel Taylor, who posted 11 interceptions and 92 receptions respectively, Denver lacked the talent of its competitors and struggled to a 4–9–1 record, the worst in the league.

After Denver slipped to 3–11 in its second season, the team hired a new coach named Jack Faulkner. In an effort to breathe life into his young club, Coach Faulkner changed the team uniforms. The new look seemed to help, as the now orange-and-blue Broncos surged to a 7–2 start in 1962. Even though the

Fans called him the "$130,000 Lemon."

team stumbled late in the season, fan attendance at home games doubled, and Faulkner was named the AFL Coach of the Year.

Unfortunately, no other Broncos season would be that successful during the rest of the 1960s. The team would be led by five different coaches during the decade, but none would guide the Broncos to a winning record. Although Denver would feature such brilliant players as running back Cookie Gilchrist and receiver Al Denson during those years, it would finish its opening decade with a collective 39–97–4 record—the worst of any of the original AFL teams.

Remarkably, despite their losing ways, the Broncos' popularity kept climbing. Starting in 1970 (the year the AFL merged with the National Football League, or NFL) and continuing for three decades, every game at Denver's Mile High Stadium would be sold out. One of the reasons for this amazing support was Denver's ability to attract exciting stars such as running back Floyd Little.

In 1967, the Broncos paid the then huge sum of $130,000 for Little, who had been a three-time All-American at Syracuse University. When he gained only 381 rushing yards his rookie year, disappointed fans called him the "$130,000 Lemon." Then, in 1968, the franchise reached a turning point. The team adopted new uniforms with a helmet that featured a bucking bronco inside of a capital D. And jeers turned to cheers as Little—running behind linemen Larry Kaminski, Bob Young, and Tom Beer—began to tear through opposing defenses. "I remember one play in one game late in that 1968 season," Little later recalled. "It wasn't the length of the run, which was short, or the game, which was just another game, but it was the execution of the play. It was perfect.... All of a sudden, all the pieces of our jigsaw puzzle were falling into place."

Despite Little's optimism, the Broncos continued to come up short in the standings, finishing 5–8–1 in both 1969 and 1970. After a poor start in 1971, general manager and head coach Lou Saban resigned, and the Broncos finished 4–9–1. Under yet another new coach, John Ralston, Denver maintained its losing ways in 1972 with a 5–9 record. Despite it all, Broncos fans continued to show up and support their team.

The Great Sock Barbecue

For decades, the Denver Broncos have been closely, and proudly, connected to the color orange. But during their first two seasons, they weren't so lucky. Short on money, the team's general manager, Dean Griffing, chose to buy used uniforms featuring yellow jerseys with numbers that matched the team's brown pants. The uniforms were ugly, but the accompanying striped socks were historically bad. After Denver went a combined 7–20–1 in its first two seasons, Jack Faulkner was brought in as the new head coach and general manager. Hoping to change their luck, the team bought new uniforms and introduced the slogan "There's lots new in '62!" Then Faulkner held a public burning of what had become the symbol of those first two dismal years: the hated socks. In front of more than 8,000 fans gathered in Denver's Bears Stadium, Broncos players marched past a replica of the Olympic flame and tossed their hated striped socks into the fire. Defensive tackle Bud McFadin echoed the thoughts of many of his teammates when he said, "They were the most ridiculous [socks] I ever saw in my life."

THE 1960 AND 1961 BRONCOS BECAME FAMOUS FOR THEIR AWFUL SOCKS

AFTER FLOYD LITTLE DEPARTED, ROB LYTLE (PICTURED) HELPED CARRY THE LOAD

After several years of disappointment, the Denver faithful finally began to feel optimistic as the 1973 season rolled around. Thanks to quarterback Charley Johnson and players such as Little and deep-threat receiver Haven Moses, fans had good reason to be hopeful. The Broncos finished 1973 with a winning record—the first in franchise history—going 7–5–2. In 1974, the team expanded the Mile High Stadium's seating capacity to 75,000 to accommodate the rapidly growing demand for tickets as the Broncos finished with their second straight winning record. Unfortunately, the next year, Denver fell to 6–8 in what proved to be Little's last season. When the player known as "The Franchise" retired in 1975, the team retired his number 44 jersey along with him.

Tom Jackson

LINEBACKER / BRONCOS SEASONS: 1973–86 / HEIGHT: 5-FOOT-11 / WEIGHT: 220 POUNDS

From the time he was a kid, Tom Jackson was told that he was too small to be a successful football player. Even after a terrific college career at the University of Louisville, he was not chosen until the fourth round of the 1973 NFL Draft. Both intelligent and dedicated, the player who was supposed to be too little became a huge part of Denver's "Orange Crush" defense of the mid-1970s. In the 1977 playoffs, the Broncos' first postseason appearance, Jackson helped his team defeat the Pittsburgh Steelers with two interceptions and a fumble recovery. His dedication made him exceptionally popular with fans, and his teammates voted him the Broncos' "Most Inspirational Player" for six consecutive seasons. "I loved to practice," he said in an interview after retiring. "I loved lying there in a puddle of sweat, exhausted and knowing that I was preparing myself as best I could to be successful on the weekend." After a 14-year NFL career, Jackson put his football knowledge to use by becoming one of the most respected NFL analysts on television.

Orange Crush

Great team units often earn great nicknames. In the late 1960s and early '70s, that was especially true with dominant defenses in the NFL. The stingy defense of the Pittsburgh Steelers was dubbed "The Steel Curtain." The ferocious attack of the Minnesota Vikings' defensive line earned it the nickname "Purple People Eaters." So when the 1977 Denver Broncos defense led the AFC in fewest points, yards, and rushing yards allowed per game, it seemed only fitting that it should have a nickname of its own. While being named after a popular soft drink, Orange Crush, may not seem too intimidating, it was certainly appropriate. The Denver defense, wearing its bright orange jerseys, consistently crushed opposing offenses with the fearsome play of defensive linemen such as Lyle Alzado and Rubin Carter and linebackers Randy Gradishar and Tom Jackson. "The Orange Crush was a nickname we enjoyed," defensive back Billy Thompson recalled. "It was a signature time in Broncos history because we moved from being a team that wasn't respectable to a team that had a chance to win."

BRONCOS FANS HAVE LONG CELEBRATED ORANGE AS A COLOR OF DOMINANCE

Broncomania Begins

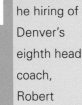

The hiring of Denver's eighth head coach, Robert "Red" Miller, in 1977 signaled the start of a new era. That era was dubbed "Broncomania" for the wild enthusiasm that filled Mile High Stadium for each Broncos home game. Coach Miller helped trigger that excitement before the 1977 season by announcing, "The Broncos will make Denver proud. We're not scared of anyone. We can beat any team."

Miller's players backed up his words, winning the franchise's first American Football Conference (AFC) West Division title with a 12–2 record. Led by veteran quarterback Craig Morton, Denver's offense was anything but explosive. But with a defense featuring huge linemen Rubin Carter and Lyle Alzado and fearless linebackers Randy Gradishar and Tom Jackson, Denver didn't need to score many points to win. Nicknamed the

LYLE ALZADO'S FEROCITY MADE HIM ONE OF THE MOST FEARED PLAYERS OF HIS DAY

Karl Mecklenburg

LINEBACKER / BRONCOS SEASONS: 1983–94 / HEIGHT: 6-FOOT-3 / WEIGHT: 240 POUNDS

Karl Mecklenburg's NFL career is one of the great Cinderella stories in league history. He was a walk-on player at the University of Minnesota, and in 1983, he waited until the 12th round of the NFL Draft before the Broncos selected him. The 310th overall pick in the draft, Mecklenburg went on to earn 6 Pro Bowl selections. After he spent one season at defensive end, the Broncos chose to capitalize on his versatile skills by moving him around a lot. Although Mecklenburg is primarily remembered as a linebacker, his athleticism encouraged coaches to put him at seven different positions on defense, many times lining him up at each one in a single game. Wherever he lined up, he was a devastating tackler and a fearsome pass rusher, notching a career high of 13 sacks in 1985. Mecklenburg's defensive leadership helped the Broncos get to three Super Bowls during his career, although they came up short in each one. As of 2013, he remained a popular figure in Colorado, dedicating much of his time to charities and motivational speaking.

"John never seemed to doubt anything."

VANCE JOHNSON
ON JOHN ELWAY

"Orange Crush" on account of its orange home jerseys and physical style of play, the Denver defense was one of the NFL's most dominant.

When the defending Super Bowl champion Oakland Raiders arrived at Mile High Stadium for the 1977 AFC Championship Game, all they could see was orange. Denver fans went wild as the Orange Crush held Oakland to a first-half field goal, and the Broncos won 20–17 to advance to Super Bowl XII. Unfortunately, the Broncos fell just short of a world championship, losing 27–10 to an opportunistic Dallas Cowboys defense that recovered four Denver fumbles and intercepted the ball four times.

ith its crushing defense still dominating opponents, Denver powered its way to the playoffs again in 1978 with a 10–6 record. However, the Broncos' defense wasn't enough to suppress the Pittsburgh Steelers' powerful offense in the postseason, and Denver was routed 33–10. In 1979, another 10–6 record earned the team a Wild Card berth into the playoffs. This time it was the Houston Oilers that knocked the Broncos from Super Bowl contention, topping Denver 13–7. Those seasons cemented the Broncos' legacy as one of the NFL's finest teams of the late '70s, even though a world championship remained just out of reach.

After Denver faded to 8–8 in 1980, Coach Miller was replaced by Dan Reeves. A man with extensive Super Bowl experience, Reeves had played or coached in five Super Bowls with the Dallas Cowboys. When Reeves led the Broncos to an improved 10–6 mark his first year, Denver fans began dreaming of Super Bowl glory once again. But many Broncos greats of the '70s had gotten old or moved on, and Denver lacked a true star to guide it to success in the postseason.

That changed in 1983. That year's NFL Draft produced a number of quarterbacks who would become legendary stars, but the Broncos got the one every team wanted most: Stanford University standout John Elway. An All-American with a cannon for an arm and a rare ability for reading and exploiting defenses, Elway would become the decisive leader that the Broncos had been lacking.

After Denver made him the NFL's highest-paid rookie, Elway proved his worth by coolly leading the

The Drive

It was the fourth quarter of the 1986 AFC Championship Game. The Cleveland Browns were leading the visiting Denver Broncos by a score of 20–13. After a botched kickoff return, Elway and the Broncos lined up at their own two-yard line with 5:32 left on the game clock, beginning what would eventually become known simply as "The Drive." During the 15-play drive, running back Sammy Winder ran the ball 3 times for a total of 8 yards and caught 1 pass. Elway twice had to scramble for yards to keep the drive alive. He went to the air 9 times, hitting receivers Steve Watson and Mark Jackson and running back Steve Sewell for 5 passes, including a 5-yard touchdown strike to Jackson to tie the game with 31 seconds remaining. The Drive kept the Broncos in the game and gave them the chance they needed to win it with a field goal in overtime. "Being human," wide receiver Vance Johnson said afterwards, "you tend to doubt yourself at times. But John never seemed to doubt anything at the end."

"THE DRIVE" EARNED JOHN ELWAY AND THE BRONCOS A PLACE IN NFL LORE

DAN REEVES AND JOHN ELWAY LED THE BRONCOS TOGETHER FOR 10 SEASONS

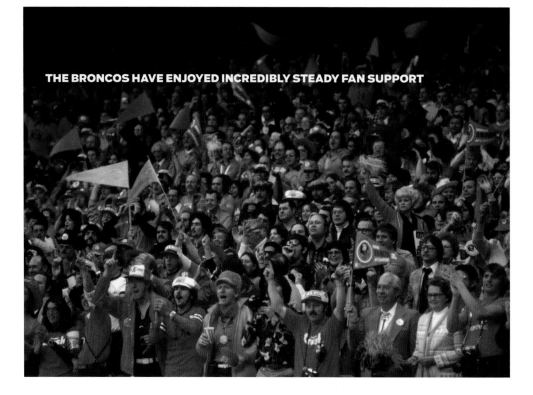

THE BRONCOS HAVE ENJOYED INCREDIBLY STEADY FAN SUPPORT

Broncos to the playoffs in 1983. Then, in 1984, the young quarterback guided Denver to the AFC West title with a 13–3 mark. Whether he was launching a deep pass, firing up his teammates, or scrambling for a big gain, Elway expected a lot from himself. "My goal is to beat [Hall of Fame Steelers quarterback] Terry Bradshaw," Elway said. "He won the Super Bowl four times. I want to win five."

The Broncos made quick exits from the playoffs in 1983 and 1984. Although the team missed the playoffs in 1985, Elway put on a great show, throwing for 3,891 yards and 22 touchdowns, with many of those passes going to receiver Vance Johnson. That was just the start of one of the most remarkable careers in NFL history. In all, the quarterback in the number 7 jersey would spend 16 seasons in the "Mile-High City," passing for more than 3,000 yards in 12 of them. In the 10 years (1983–1992) that Denver had coach Dan Reeves on the sidelines and John Elway under center, the Broncos would suffer just 1 losing season and make the playoffs 6 times.

The Broncos Get It Done

As the Broncos took the field against the Green Bay Packers after the 1997 season in Super Bowl XXXII, it was in hopes of becoming the first AFC team since the 1983 Los Angeles Raiders to become world champions. From the kickoff, the two teams traded scores as well as turnovers. At halftime, Denver led 17–14, but the Packers tied the game with a field goal early in the third quarter. The Broncos came back with a drive of their own that was highlighted by a scramble and dive by Elway to set up a first-and-goal situation. That was all Terrell Davis needed as he took the ball into the end zone on the next play. After the two teams traded touchdowns in the fourth quarter, the Packers, down 31–24, were shut down by the Broncos' defense, and Super Bowl XXXII belonged to the Broncos and the AFC. Davis earned Most Valuable Player (MVP) honors as he overcame a severe migraine headache to tally 157 yards and 3 touchdowns in the game. "For all the Broncos fans who never had this feeling," said Elway, "we finally got it done."

DENVER CELEBRATED BIG PLAYS IN THE LATE '90s WITH THE "MILE-HIGH SALUTE"

RICH KARLIS KICKED SEVEN FIELD GOALS IN ONE 1989 GAME

The Elway Era

In the late 1980s, new defensive stars emerged in Denver, including linebacker Karl Mecklenburg and safety Dennis Smith. Yet it was Elway who remained the driving force behind the Broncos. As he led the team into the postseason in 1986, 1987, and 1989, he became known as a "comeback king" because of his knack for rallying the Broncos on game-winning drives late in the fourth quarter.

One such drive took place in the AFC Championship Game after the 1986 season. Trailing the Cleveland Browns 20–13 with just five and a half minutes left in the game, the Broncos got the ball on their own two-yard line. Facing a tough Browns defense, a rowdy Cleveland crowd, and a stiff wind, Elway completed one pressure-packed pass after another to drive Denver the length of the field for the tying touchdown. Broncos kicker Rich Karlis, who famously always kicked with a bare foot, then booted a field goal for a 23–20 overtime victory, earning Denver a berth in Super Bowl XXI against the New York Giants. Unfortunately for Denver fans, the Giants were loaded with talent that year and crushed the Broncos, 39–20.

JOHN ELWAY HAD FAST FEET, GREAT FIELD VISION, AND A POWERFUL RIGHT ARM

✗John Elway

QUARTERBACK / BRONCOS SEASONS: 1983–98 / HEIGHT: 6-FOOT-3 / WEIGHT: 215 POUNDS

When time was running out and the Broncos needed to score, John Elway was at his best. Although he had a powerful passing arm and elusive scrambling ability, he was best known for his ability to rally his team late in games. In total, Elway orchestrated 47 fourth-quarter, game-winning or game-tying drives. In the 1986 AFC title game, he led his team on a 98-yard comeback drive to help beat the Cleveland Browns with a legendary rally that is still known simply as "The Drive." Although he was one of the most respected quarterbacks in the league for more than a decade, Elway's resumé wasn't complete until Super Bowl XXXII, after the 1997 season, when the Broncos won the first of two consecutive Super Bowls behind his leadership. "The thing that was so impressive to me was the concentration level and the poise in thriving on pressure," said former Broncos coach Mike Shanahan. "He knew and believed that he was so prepared, so physically in shape, that if he was put in that situation, he would win."

GARY ZIMMERMAN MADE HIS FIRST PRO BOWL AT AGE 26 AND LAST AT 35

he Broncos rebounded from that loss by marching right back to the Super Bowl in 1987 and 1989. Denver fans were again left broken-hearted by the outcomes, though. After the Broncos were crushed by the Washington Redskins, 42–10, and the San Francisco 49ers, 55–10, some critics wondered if Denver would ever win the big game. But even as the team put together some mediocre seasons in the early 1990s, Elway and new stars such as sure-handed tight end Shannon Sharpe and hard-hitting safety Steve Atwater gave fans hope.

In 1995, the Broncos made two key moves that would finally take them to the top. First, they hired Mike Shanahan—the offensive coordinator for the 49ers team that had beaten the Broncos in Super Bowl XXIV—as the franchise's 11th head coach. Then, in the 1995 NFL Draft, the Broncos found a hidden gem. With the 196th pick, they selected University of Georgia running back Terrell Davis. Called "T. D." by his teammates, Davis quickly gave the Broncos a deadly rushing attack.

In 1996, as linemen Gary Zimmerman and Brian Habib paved the way, Davis charged for 1,538 yards. Behind this sensational effort, the Broncos went 13–3 and won their division before losing to the Jacksonville Jaguars in a playoff upset. Denver dug deeper in 1997 as Davis exploded for 1,750 yards on the season, and young receiver Rod Smith emerged as a big-play threat to help Denver reach its fifth Super Bowl. This time, Denver faced the defending Super Bowl champion Green Bay Packers in the big game.

With the game tied 24–24 in the fourth quarter, Elway led yet another sensational drive, marching Denver down the field. Then, with less than two minutes remaining, Davis plunged into the end zone to finally give the Broncos their first world championship. "I'm so proud and happy that we could win this for Denver fans

TERRELL DAVIS BULLED HIS WAY TO THREE TOUCHDOWNS IN SUPER BOWL XXXII

Running in the Zone

Between 1994 and 2007, the Denver Broncos had 6 different running backs reach the 1,000-yard mark, and Terrell Davis even eclipsed the hallowed 2,000-yard barrier in 1998. Year after year, Denver running backs were among the league leaders. The reason that Denver's running game was so successful could be explained largely by a zone blocking scheme installed by offensive line coach Alex Gibbs. Instead of offensive linemen such as tackle Gary Zimmerman and center Tom Nalen locking up man-to-man with defensive players, they worked together to open up one side of the line. The running back's job was to find the first available hole and make one sharp cut through it to gain yards. The result was that running backs such as Clinton Portis and Mike Anderson were able to waste less time waiting for their assigned hole to open up and consistently pick up positive yardage. The zone blocking scheme relied on smart, mobile linemen and running backs who could explode through the gaps. Although the Broncos made zone blocking famous, several teams in the NFL soon adopted the technique.

CLINTON PORTIS REACHED THE END ZONE A COMBINED 31 TIMES IN 2002 AND 2003

OFFENSIVE LINEMAN TONY JONES PROTECTED ELWAY HIS LAST TWO SEASONS

and for John," said Davis. "John Elway has meant everything to this franchise, and it's so great to see him finally get what he deserves."

**D**enver fans found more reasons for celebration the next season. After Davis became the fourth running back in NFL history to rush for more than 2,000 yards in a season, the Broncos galloped back to the Super Bowl. In what turned out to be Elway's farewell performance, the Hall of Fame quarterback passed for 336 yards in a 34–19 victory over the Atlanta Falcons. After the game, Elway announced his retirement, ending his brilliant career while on top of the football world.

Life after Elway proved to be a difficult adjustment for the Broncos—an adjustment made all the more challenging as Davis suffered a series of injuries that limited his playing time and effectiveness. The defending Super Bowl champs managed just six victories in 1999. The following year, they reached the playoffs but were pummeled 21–3 in the first round by the eventual champion Baltimore Ravens.

In 2001, the Broncos moved from their longtime home of Mile High Stadium into the newly constructed Invesco Field at Mile High. The change in venue did little to improve the team's fortunes, however, as Denver narrowly missed the playoffs each of the following two seasons.

"EASY ED" McCAFFREY WAS ONE OF ELWAY'S MOST RELIABLE PASSING TARGETS

AL WILSON HAD A WELL-EARNED REPUTATION AS A PUNISHING HITTER

Trial and Error

Heading into the 2003 season, Denver fans were optimistic the Broncos could return to championship form. The team brought in former Arizona Cardinals quarterback Jake "The Snake" Plummer, whose confidence, quick feet, and knack for orchestrating comeback victories reminded many fans of Elway. He was paired with running back Clinton Portis, who had delighted fans and inspired teammates by rushing for 1,508 yards and had earned Offensive Rookie of the Year honors in 2002.

Injuries limited Plummer's playing time in 2003, but Portis further established himself as an elite rusher, tallying 1,591 yards. Meanwhile, the Broncos defense, anchored by run-stuffing middle linebacker Al Wilson, was the stingiest it had been since Denver's Super Bowl seasons. With a 10–6 record, the Broncos earned a Wild Card playoff slot. Unfortunately, they were outmatched by quarterback Peyton Manning and the high-scoring Indianapolis Colts, who torched Denver 41–10 in a blowout.

Following this defensive embarrassment, the Broncos traded Portis to the

DENVER CONTINUED TO BUILD UP ITS DEFENSE BY ADDING END ELVIS DUMERVIL

✕Shannon Sharpe

TIGHT END / BRONCOS SEASONS: 1990–99, 2002–03 / HEIGHT: 6-FOOT-2 / WEIGHT: 228 POUNDS

When Shannon Sharpe was on the football field, everyone knew it. One of the most notorious (and comedic) trash talkers in NFL history, he was also a vital part of the Broncos' championship-caliber offense in both 1997 and 1998. Drafted as a wide receiver, Sharpe played very little early in his first season, and because of his size, he was used as a tight end during practices. Once the Denver coaching staff realized that he had a knack for getting open and catching passes from that position, they gave him his chance. Sharpe became quarterback John Elway's favorite target in clutch situations and developed a reputation of holding on to passes even while taking big hits. After a 14-year career, he retired as the NFL's all-time leader in receptions and receiving yards among tight ends. "I've always liked to talk, and it's who I am," he said at his retirement. After he hung up his cleats, Sharpe used his gift for gab as an NFL analyst on *The NFL Today* pregame show on CBS. Sharpe was inducted into the Pro Football Hall of Fame in 2011.

Washington Redskins for lock-down cornerback Champ Bailey and added John Lynch, a tough and crafty safety. However, after a healthy Plummer led Denver to another 10–6 record and playoff berth in 2004, the Colts once again overwhelmed the Broncos defense, this time blowing Denver out 49–24.

In 2005, the defense bounced back, Plummer had his most efficient season yet, and instead of a single rushing threat, Denver relied on two contrasting running backs. The grinding Mike Anderson and darting Tatum Bell combined to rush for 20 touchdowns and nearly 2,000 yards. With the team firing on all cylinders, the Broncos put together the second-best record in the AFC at 13–3 and defeated the defending champion New England Patriots in the playoffs. The Broncos then hosted the Steelers in the AFC Championship Game.

BRANDON MARSHALL WAS AMONG THE NFL'S MOST IMPOSING RECEIVERS

Unfortunately, Plummer committed four turnovers, and the Steelers won 34–17 before going on to defeat the Seattle Seahawks in Super Bowl XL.

Denver appeared primed for another postseason run in 2006, winning seven of its first nine games. But then, after a pair of disappointing losses, Coach Shanahan replaced Plummer with rocket-armed rookie quarterback Jay Cutler for the remainder of the season. Cutler posted impressive stats but was one win short of leading Denver into the playoffs.

The down times continued for the Broncos as they struggled to a 7–9 record in 2007. Still, Cutler continued to show promise, and Brandon Marshall emerged as a physically dominating wideout, snagging 102 catches for 1,325 yards. At 230 pounds, Marshall seemed to seek out would-be tacklers rather than avoid them. As one opposing cornerback noted, "He wants to inflict punishment on you."

The passing attack continued to impress in 2008, but after the Broncos missed the playoffs for a third straight year, Shanahan was fired. The departure of the winningest coach in team history left large shoes to fill, but the Broncos' front office believed the man for the job was Josh McDaniels, a former offensive coordinator and quarterbacks coach for the potent Patriots.

McDaniels wasted no time in shaking things up, dealing Cutler away to the Chicago Bears for unspectacular but steady quarterback Kyle Orton and three high draft selections. The trade received mixed reactions from the Denver faithful, but nearing the midpoint of the 2009 season, the front office appeared to have made all the right moves, as the Broncos won each of their first six games. However, the mile-high Broncos then came back to Earth, losing seven of the next nine games. Denver still had

Tebowmania

Quarterback Tim Tebow enjoyed great success at the collegiate level, but his unorthodox throwing mechanics and "run-first" mentality kept him sidelined for most of his first pro season. But after Denver struggled to begin the 2011 season, Tebow started the Week 7 matchup against the Miami Dolphins. He looked shaky most of the game but threw two touchdown passes in the final three minutes, setting up an overtime victory. Still, football analysts said Tebow was too unpolished to continue winning. Those critics were soon eating their words. Tebow's passing numbers weren't great, but his running skills, careful protection of the ball, and late-game heroics boosted the Broncos to an unlikely six-game winning streak. His fame rose as he continuously proved doubters wrong, and his rugged looks, personable nature, and unabashed displays of his Christian faith endeared him to fans outside the mainstream sports world. "Tebowmania" peaked when he capped a postseason upset over the Steelers with an overtime touchdown pass. The following off-season was bittersweet for Broncos fans, however. Denver signed future Hall-of-Famer Peyton Manning, but many Tebowmaniacs were saddened when Tebow was subsequently traded to the New York Jets.

TIM TEBOW BECAME ONE OF THE BIGGEST FIGURES IN ALL OF SPORTS IN 2011

PLAYING IN SNOWY DENVER, THE BRONCOS HAVE LONG RELIED ON STRONG RUSHING

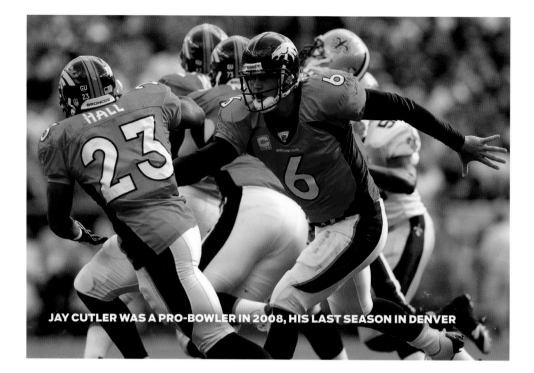

JAY CUTLER WAS A PRO-BOWLER IN 2008, HIS LAST SEASON IN DENVER

a chance to make the playoffs if it won its season finale. But more controversy arose when McDaniels benched Marshall for the pivotal game for disciplinary reasons. Denver lost the game, and Marshall was traded away before the next season. After the disappointing 2009 finish, the wheels fell off in 2010 as Denver lost a franchise record 12 games. Near season's end, McDaniels was fired.

Heading into the 2011 season, the Broncos' home stadium was renamed Sports Authority Field at Mile High, and the defense-oriented John Fox was hired as head coach. The Broncos struggled to a 1–4 start, but hope was rekindled as Orton was replaced by young backup quarterback Tim Tebow. In college, Tebow had helped the University of Florida Gators win two national titles, and although unproven in the NFL, the brawny, mobile quarterback with a history of winning was an appealing prospect. Helping him out was fellow second-year player Eric Decker—a big target at wide receiver with a nose for the end zone. On the other side of the ball, rookie linebacker Von Miller quickly earned a reputation as a disruptive defender, racking up six sacks during his first six games as a pro. The Broncos finished the season as the league's top-ranked running offense and made the playoffs for the first time in six years.

In the playoffs, Denver hosted the defending AFC champion Steelers. After Denver managed only eight total yards in the first quarter, the Broncos surged back and took a 20–6 lead before halftime. The resilient Steelers answered in the second half, tying the game at 23–23 and forcing overtime. Pittsburgh seemed to have momentum on its side, but Denver won the coin toss and received the ball. On the very first play from scrimmage, wide receiver Demaryius Thomas caught an 18-yard pass, shoved off a defender, and ran another 62 yards for the game-winning touchdown.

Mike Shanahan

COACH / BRONCOS SEASONS: 1995–2008

Between 1995 and 2008, no head coach in the NFL won more games than the Broncos' Mike Shanahan. After taking over on the sidelines for Denver in 1995, it took this personable yet highly disciplined leader only two years to bring a Super Bowl title to the Mile-High City. Using a run-focused variation on the "West Coast Offense" that he helped to develop as an offensive coordinator with the San Francisco 49ers, Shanahan made the Broncos into one of the most prolific scoring teams in the history of the NFL. Although Shanahan wasn't a coach who gave the media a lot of insight into his plans or his thoughts, his openness with his team made him a popular and trusted leader in the locker room and on the sidelines. His success earned the respect of his teams as well as his peers. "Mike Shanahan is one of the best," said Mike Holmgren, former head coach of the Seattle Seahawks. "Everyone knows it. He's very disciplined, very thorough.… His teams play very hard." After leaving Denver, Shanahan became head coach of the Washington Redskins.

PEYTON MANNING INSTANTLY TURNED THE BRONCOS INTO A CONTENDER IN 2012

VON MILLER LED DENVER'S DEFENSE WITH HIS RELENTLESS PASS RUSHING

The Broncos lost the following week to the Patriots, but hope had been rekindled in Denver. That spark of hope burst into flames of optimism in the off-season when Denver landed veteran free agent quarterback Peyton Manning—a perennial All-Pro and longtime tormentor of the Broncos. The move made Denver an immediate Super Bowl contender. "We're going to do whatever we can to win right now," said Manning.

"Whatever" needed more than a month to become apparent as the Broncos opened the season 2–3. Starting in Week 6 with a 35–24 win over the San Diego Chargers, the Broncos ran the table to end with an AFC-best 13–3 mark. Manning silenced all doubters by having one of his best seasons ever, throwing for 4,659 yards and 37 touchdowns. In the playoffs, the Broncos seemed to have the Ravens in hand, holding a 35–28 lead with 31 seconds left and Baltimore at their own 30-yard line. But a defensive breakdown allowed a game-tying, 70-yard touchdown pass to sail through. Then Manning threw for an interception in the second overtime, which led to a Ravens field goal. Shockingly, Denver's season was over in a flash. Maintaining his trademark professional attitude, Manning met reporters after the game. "You want it to work and keep going and win, but that's not always the way it works," he said.

Like the mountains of Colorado, the Broncos' history has had its share of peaks and valleys. From bottom-dwelling beginnings, Denver has determinedly fought to climb ever higher, creating such memorable highlights as the "Orange Crush" defense and "The Drive" as they came up just short of the summit. Denver fans beamed with pride when John Elway and the Broncos finally stood tall atop the NFL as world champions. Although setbacks and controversies brought them back down out of the clouds in the past decade, today's Broncos are primed to scale their next mountain.

INDEX